UNTIL THE FULL MOON HAS ITS SAY

MADE IN MICHIGAN WRITERS SERIES

GENERAL EDITORS

Michael Delp, *Interlochen Center for the Arts*

M. L. Liebler, *Wayne State University*

ADVISORY EDITORS

Melba Joyce Boyd, *Wayne State University*

Stuart Dybek, *Western Michigan University*

Kathleen Glynn

Jerry Herron, *Wayne State University*

Laura Kasischke, *University of Michigan*

Thomas Lynch

Frank Rashid, *Marygrove College*

Doug Stanton

Keith Taylor, *University of Michigan*

*A complete listing of the books in this series
can be found online at* **wsupress.wayne.edu**

UNTIL THE FULL MOON HAS ITS SAY

Poems by CONRAD HILBERRY

 Wayne State University Press | *Detroit*

18 17 16 15 14   5 4 3 2 1

ISBN 978-0-8143-4024-0 (paperback) / ISBN 978-0-8143-4025-7 (e-book)

Library of Congress Control Number: 2013944708

∞

Publication of this book was made possible by a generous gift from The Meijer Foundation.

Designed and typeset by Charlie Sharp, Sharp Des!gns, Lansing, Michigan
Composed in Adobe Minion

For my family

CONTENTS

ACKNOWLEDGMENTS

"Schooled in the Open Sea," "Divertimento 563," and "Mosquitoes" were previously published in the *Hudson Review*.

"Virginia Night" and "Let It Be Night" first appeared in *Dunes Review*.

"February," "Algae," "Garlic Mustard," and "Divertimento 563" (reprint) appeared in *Encore Magazine*.

Special thanks to all of the poets in the Sunday Group.

One

April

April takes down my love—
wrong season for dying.
Even the box elder,
hunching into the clouds,
is blooming, branching,
leaving.
          She's leaving,
half-aware in the tilted bed,
breath barely coming,
then not. Jaws
clamped around a scrap
of tongue. Her warm body
gone cooler, cold.
Hospice to wash her.
Two mortuary men.

What had been touch
and talk, ripe fruit,
red wine:
a stalk
in a winter field.

Villanelle for Marion

My glass was empty then.
Barmaid, lift the spigot, let it run.
Still empty. Then a dark-haired one

found me under some banyan
tree, imagining love, alone.
My glass was empty then.

She knew the January sky, and June,
had a touch to nudge the season—
empty, full. I'll take the dark-haired one.

She knew the streets of Paris, London,
hitchhiked south along the Seine,
finding no glass empty then.

We cooked up lunch in Madison,
two-handled bowl of bluefin,
noodles, peas—a savory one

to feed the co-op. Found a path down
to Lake Mendota, spring rain,
swamp grass, no glass empty then—
dipper full, the spring, a dark-haired one.

Memory

Everything that was—touch
football in the street, Peggy

McKay in the hay wagon,
Miss LaBatt's geometry, the second

floor in Madison, where
one daughter slept in a closet.

Is any of this true? Nightgowns,
glances, griefs existing nowhere

but in this sieve of memory.
Newspaper files, bank accounts,

court records—nothing there.
It's gone, except for these scratchy

words—blackbird on a branch,
long story caught in his throat.

Limbs

Outside the window of the gallery,
dead branches etch a slow-moving

cloud, black against a shifty white.
How can I draw dead branches

in a poem? A skillful pen or brush
could do it with a few dark strokes.

Words want to say the branches
writhe or ache. They don't.

They're dead wood, left over
in the sky, the past hung up,

peeled to the bone.

Bowl

On the bed in the dining room—
half herself, half emptiness,

lovely bowl, without any gestures,
any goodbyes, she lets go, lets

everything she has been drift out,
slip from the bed to the floor—

those years of touching, listening—
like a blanket, a sheet,

breath, words, whispers
finding their way down and out,

not explaining, dropping
whatever she held in her hand.

January on the Pond

Iced in, a goldfish floats, eye open,
nudging a rock—gills, fins, orange

scales lapping the sides. We all
winter down, glass-eyed.

Question: Will that fish twist
and leap when the cold breaks?

Hunch and stare fixed as granite.
But who knows? When April

nods to the weeders and planters,
will that fish shiver, nose to tail,

let the scales breathe? Can the sun
call back an eye, a heart?

Empty Plate

I take off my glasses, let my face
go long, one eye half-closed,

mouth slightly open. That's the face
itself, not me. When did we drift apart?

Where had I been keeping this
drawn-out mask, when I

taught and loved, even held
an audience in my hand?

Somewhere, just behind my skeptical
nod in class, I'd stored away

this empty plate, hoping
never to open up the cupboard.

The Surge

Those were watery epochs, breathing
salt, nudging our scales into the murk.
Then Mama inched her belly up the sand

and took a sip of air. Come on up.
We liked it where we were, but no,
up it was. Fins morphed to hands,

tails to feet, we crawled. She was right,
we didn't need to nibble plankton,
dodge the carp, eat our cousin minnows.

Breakfast was everywhere—six legs
limping on clay, four wings forgetting
our quick tongues. We ate, we mated,

multiplied. But when the sun sinks,
I sink with it, back to the surge
where everything began.

Sadness

Our clear Virginia sky's gone
gloomy, dark. Now if sadness

sits cross-legged under some tree,
who will notice? The wind itself is sad.

•

Why these short sentences,
half a tongue at a time?
Depression, grief, remorse—

they roll right out, saw down
the family tree, dig a six-foot
hole if things are bad.

But sadness sings half a tune,
undoes a braid, lets the tide
edge up around the hips.

•

Chevy handed down needs a new transmission.
That's the word. So come touch a fender,

wipe off the tail light. Remember that first drive—
the shimmy-skinned back seat? How much

are they asking for those years again?

•

Heart in the back seat, Marjorie says. Heart
in a jar. I'd like mine to find a shadowed

corner on the windowsill—or hang
from a doorknob like the purse

some earringed woman left behind.
Instead, it sits at the narrow table

spooning its soft-boiled yolk.

●

Death at the proper time brings
sadness with it on the gurney—

down the aisle, pause at the altar,
into the hole. But death-too-soon—

a nine-year daughter gone
in a Spanish night—that's grief.

Click

Padlock closing. Or the door
of the cell block. Let it be

the grandfather clock
near the front door,

two weights hanging,
one to nudge the seconds,

one to bong out the children's
years, the parents' emptiness.

It's October here, not far
from the end. I'm listening,

lawn mower a block away,
train rattle blown in

from the north,
nothing conclusive

but the click of a bug
camped out in the shagbark.

Vein and Muscle

My neighbor spotted it in the August woods,
a red-tailed hawk, beak hooking up strands of meat
from some new kill, neck stretched, sucking the goods.
Wildest bird in our hickory swamp, she ate,
looked up, stretched her four-foot wings, and rose
dodging through our brush and branches. Gone.
I checked to see what animal she chose
to claw down and devour. Black squirrel, torn
at the throat, breast flesh stripped away.

A sonnet-sized event, a few lines left
for us watchers to pause, recall a painful day . . .
No, not in my poem. No metaphoric theft.
This story is winged hunger, swoop and spur,
and a rope of vein and muscle fletched from its fur.

Virginia Night

Virginia night with stars, not much to do
but lose the path and watch Orion rise.
Supposed to be a comet coming through.

When sun is up, we feel obliged to hew
some timber, show some enterprise.
Then comes Virginia night, the deepest blue.

One fist of stars is faintly clear when you
look somewhere else—then they vanish, vaporize
like the promised comet that's not passing through.

The dipper spills its emptiness into
my cup. No need. My pitcher's twice that size.
Virginia night and stars, they drink it too.

Solitude and night may help me brew
the juice to freshen memory, what lies
just out of reach, a comet passing through.

Some lovely lives have vanished, one or two,
their shadows on the walk, their arms, their eyes.
The night, the stars, they've done what they can do.
There might still be a comet passing through.

Two

Blackout

No light outside or in,
no moon, no stars.
No murmur from the fridge.

We know our manufactured dark,
the dark to dance in, sleep in,
dark where old resentments

roil or sometimes melt.
This dark has washed away
the desk, the screen, the window

and its woods, the words
we might be saying.
This is the emptiness

where everything began.

Schooled in the Open Sea

The albacore, bonita, mackerel
that school by millions in the open sea
are sloping off, just this side of nil.

Those oily muscles fishers used to sell
in seaside towns and then the A and P—
albacore, bonita, mackerel—

the iridescent skin and forking tail,
are netted now by dry-land industry.
The numbers slide, just this side of nil.

Tunas so large their blood runs warm, not cool,
are lifted from their deep geography,
as are the albacore, the mackerel.

Of no significance to any pool
of vertebrates, any menagerie,
I, too, am sloping off, this side of nil,

but there the likeness ends. Natural
my slant is. I don't ask the company
of albacore, bonita, mackerel.
I'll wane alone—my path to nil.

Danse Macabre

Don't study the moves. They'll come—
the lurch, the hunch, the shoulder roll,
the stare into some widow's eyes

there by the post. Get out on the floor.
Everybody's tired of two-steps—all
sambaed out. Listen: Water reaching

over in its bed. Some rumbled
out of that gulch behind the barn.
Aren't you supposed to have a partner?

Pick one with the right tilt, somebody
you used to know, eyes like penlights
looking for a key lost in the drawer.

Yes, they dance, the skeletons,
and so must you, elbows out, spine
sighing, hoping the body may remember

a surge, a loving rub, a whirlwind
dusting the windows with sperm.
Fall should be the season, dark

edging in, spiders hiding in the piled
leaves, moles digging in from the cold.
But macabre listens for the throaty frog

in green water. Whatever burrows, hums
or mutters, noses up from the muck,
whatever follows the wild fires,

macabre will dance with her.

Jack of Spades

You thought I was a man. They painted
that mustache
on my lip, curled my fingers

around a spear stuck in the ground. But
wait a minute.
Look at that black heart

upside down, graceful edges curving
to a point. I began
as the Queen of Hearts,

but it didn't feel right, all those knights
sidling up, bringing
gardenias, suggesting we go

down for tea at the folly by the lake.
I didn't need
a folly. I wanted oars, salt

creeping through the cracks, an island
pulling up its roots,
floating northeast, deep water

where the sun came up. King of Diamonds
gesturing with his
crooked finger? No thanks.

I'd rather watch the six of clubs whack
the shell of a tortoise
and grill the skimpy flesh over

a twig fire behind his hut. That sixer has
rolling balls, unlike
some royalty I could name.

Scarlet to burned-out rose to black, Queen
morphed to a Jack
of my own making, smooth,

hoisted on a prick I drew myself.

Handwork

The anesthesiologist
was pleased
to take my case.

Professional. He checked
my paperwork,
raised my arm, and slipped

his needle in my armpit.
His juice decked
every scrap of nerve,

shoulder to fingertip.
The surgeon went to work,
sliced my palm,

untangled the fascia ropes,
those knots and tails
that twisted my grip.

His moves were calm
and shrewd, scraping,
scooping. All done,

cleaned out, restored.
A handbell choir
of nurses bundled me

to the wrist,
a yeasty loaf
just lifted from the fire.

Jeff brought me home,
I slept, ate, felt OK
except that now,

twelve hours after surgery,
my arm is not my own.
Out of its sling,

it flops, slides down,
falls off my knee.
I touch its lukewarm skin,

hold it, swing it up
against my stomach.
Down again

over the edge of the chair,
a water snake
hanging from a limb.

I place it on
the table—
an aborted relative

of mine?
I know it, need it.
I rock the limp thing

on my chest, stroke
its leg, scratch
the gauzy knit

of its head. It's my
slender sister, born with me
but in another room,

the one they stripped
and sent out eyeless
in the rain.

Mosquitoes

Mosquitoes have evolved. They used to fly up,
hairy, a half inch long. They'd circle
once or twice, buzzing, looking for the ripest

spot to draw my blood. I'd listen, figure out
where that sucker might be digging in,
and swat. Blood on my collar. That was forty

years ago. Now they're small, they don't
take risks, don't buzz, don't circle.
From over in some bush, they pick their strip

of neck or ankle and go straight for it.
First thing, you know, you're itching. You might
swat one now and then, but they hardly seem

worth the trouble, tiny sharpshooters zinging in
to suck a drop or two and disappear.
Mosquitoes are what I study lately, not

John Donne, not Whitehead's metaphysics,
no rocky outcrop on the Isle of Crete,
no newborn student stanzas almost

making sense. Instead, the six-legged wildlife
in these woods, a door to evolution
honing all its creatures down.

Subtract the Digits

Take any number, let's say 57,
then subtract the digits, 5 and 7,
leaving 45. That number

will always be a multiple of 9,
no matter how large or strange
the original number is: 77777?

Then 77742, divisible by 9.
I'm amazed, but probably
shouldn't be. Coincidences

lurk behind the math-prone leaves
of every rhododendron. Take
the salutatorian from your class,

subtract a math instructor
with a limp and breakfast at
the Ragged Edge, she'll be digging

rutabagas on her grandma's
farm in North Dakota. Take
a red-haired boy, subtract

a brother and a bike that coasts
in any gear, he'll be roasting
boney mackerel on the fire.

Take me, a condo dweller
by Asylum Lake. Subtract
a wife and all the slanting words

that start with Q, I'll hitch
a ride in a pickup truck,
shrugging to slurred music

in the southbound lane.

Loping Road

A quatrain never knows just when
to pitch it in. Your sonnet
lays out its eight-by-six, tells
the iamb crew to work on it—

hauls in a metaphor or two,
some rhymes, preferably not
too tedious, and by three
this afternoon you've earned a shot

of vodka at the pub, a round
of golf, supper with Lorraine,
possibly the beach. But think
of us who push an endless quatrain

up the hill with no idea
where or how to let it die.
Here comes a shifty undercover
line or two, subversive or shy

the way they used to be—then
silences that hang like Spanish
moss from a barren limb. Words,
like an urgent twist of smoke, vanish.

So, quatrain, let's shut it down,
fourth line closing on beat three
this time. Think of a suitable rhyme:
Steep words, remember me.

No, ending can't be that easy.
We're here, quatrain, still on the move.
I'll kick the starter on my motor-
bike, listen to it rev

ready to go. We'll follow the loping
road that valleys toward the bay—
holding that last rhyme off, at least
until the full moon has its say.

A Body in Between

Above the narrow road, a sky of starlings
circle like a ragged whirlwind settling
in the fractaled branches of three oaks.

They splash their black ink on the canopy—
right for this Day of the Dead. Dark music, too,
a cloud of *caws*, no tune, no timing,

just the metallic rasp. Now all at once
they lift from the oaks, a school of fish
unanimous as though they felt the season

going and knew those hickories over there
would warm their feet. Down below,
two black horses stand exactly still,

giving that random world up there
something it can count on—eight legs,
two necks, both aimed northwest. I offer

a body in between. Not that shapeless
surge, moved by some blue magnetism.
Not those sure-hooved shapes that *know*.

My skeleton pays homage to the Day.
Muscles nod to the hickories,
now the birds have left. My veins salute
the horses, who follow with their eyes
as I walk by to supper.

Angles

A dragonfly keeps coming back
to the same dead twig, a vertical one.
His body goes down diagonal,
wings horizontal in the sun.

How have the angles drifted off,
leaving my tendons tangling
like twisted vines on a shagbark tree?
Where's my transparent wing?

Let It Be Night

Blix handed me five years.
Four I've chewed up,
tossed away.

•

I'm pedaling my Raleigh, spokes
in the wind, mottled music
easing off toward evening.

Just gone yellow, a forsythia
stretches from mud where no one
planted it, leans left

as though it hears
a scrap of talk on the road.

•

A baffle of green,
darkening,
November closing the store.

That's three months of my twelve.
Nine to go.
Maybe I get reborn once more.

•

I'm watching for a hole
in the clouds and the sudden
scarred face of the moon.

•

My love's slow breath rasped
across her lips in her last hour,
asking,
almost shaping a word.

•

If I come new next summer,
let it be my
skinny self, watching by the tracks
as boxcars rumble their tonnage
west, shaking
the clay. Let it be night.

Under a streetlight, let three girls
be talking, sorting
shadows long in the grass.

Three

Abandon

Breakers peel white as they see
the end coming. Days of dip
and slouch in the wind

all the way from Sheboygan,
deep blue, no salt, a lurch
as the current shifts. Wave-head

tosses back its hair, nods
to the muscled shore. Then
beach—like this one.

You can't think of anything
to say. Feet sink in. A green
itch of weeds at the top of the dune

and downwind absence.
It should be grill and cold Molson,
Frisbee caught in the updraft,

creek dodging crooked rocks,
boots in the ashes of a wood fire.
Instead, broken water

and this sky of mine, hung
on a bare-branched oak.

Sloth

If I write a villanelle today, it's got
to lift the leaves and find its own
sad rhymes. It's raining out. It's cold. I'm not

about to poke around in this bare plot,
hoping I might spoon up a bleached-out bone,
some Saxon thing the villanelle forgot.

Plenty of rhymes—*shot, jot, apricot.*
My part is listening for a certain tone
underneath the iambs' teeter-tot.

No one pays me to stir this formal pot
and other things are waiting to be done.
But the villanelle recalls what I forgot,

that words are watching for a six-winged thought,
newly hatched, airborn, not a clone.
It could be hovering right above this spot,

an insect with translucent wings, a knot
of overlapping lines, patterns known
to merge with night like oil of bergamot.
Yes, villanelle, that's what I forgot.

Viola

I like the feel of fingers
and the bow. I get the notes right, not too much
vibrato. On stage, the violin

nods, strokes, and we're off,
strange entanglements that Mozart sewed in there.
Now she rises

right off the score, surges, circles
the room catching a scrap of sunlight in her hair.
I repeat, I comment

down here in the shade Then the cello
steps off a pier, stretches long strokes into the waves,
dives, comes back up,

raises his arms to celebrate the wind,
then dives again. Meanwhile, someone has to
row the boat,

be there to lift him out of the surf.

Julia Elsas, "untitled 2009," fabric, thread

Seen close, it's a forest of vertical
strings, darker or lighter. Stepping back,

it becomes a swooping lower lip, shadowed
below, then a hollow with a glimpse

of tongue and teeth, dark upper lip
nipped in at the middle, fabric

stitched to breath and words.

Malachite

We meet at a picnic table in November sun.
She has good subjects—Arizona heat,
a lost friend, hard years up north,

father spotting a fox in the orchard,
unmentionable suicides in someone's
father's family. Tone is managed well,

a range of voices, all convincing.
She has an eye for structure.
Some suggestions: More details, images.

If you switch from *ing*'s to real verbs,
the sentences will march. The pared-down
passages are best. And metaphors—

more of those? A little fixing and the poems
will shine. That afternoon, it seeps in.
Those suicides—the person letting

no one speak of them. The seamy men
up there in Grayling. Blue scraps
in the eyes of the lost best friend.

The tunnel, the scorching sun,
malachite of a Michigan winter—
I'm editing a life.

Novelist at Night

Enough plot and character—the lean belly
wants to dance. Small waves
shimmy up

from hips to shoulders, murmuring
their Nile-born syllables.
Snake arms

threaten and withdraw, a silk
veil rustles over breasts
and shoulders,

then opens to a belly smoothly buttoned.
Her hips enjoy the pelvic sea-surge,
what they call

the Dolphin. She's not on stage, she's here,
her back to the fireplace,
before a room

of writers, composers, artists who let
their pens and brushes slide
back into the drawer

when her live flesh answers to the lifts
and twists, the low-down
undulations

of the oud and dumbek. We lean in,
think up some images: hips
left and right

are the crossing signal stopping
traffic while the train
roars through.

No, her moves stay close to home,
joints and muscles trading
their quiet gravity.

Still, we look   wondering what subtle
engine might be weaving
down that track.

Spotted Sandpiper

looks out
over the Lake

to see what
might be waiting.

A freighter inching
toward the Soo,

two gulls on a rock,
a flock of yellowlegs,

heads down, tails up,
nabbing a meal.

A kestrel drops
to take him,

but the piper
goes for the water,

dives, swims the seaweed
like a fish. Hawk gone,

he flies straight up,
water to air. All

the elements but fire,
he owns them.

Garlic Mustard

It's up, an early riser, stretching,
unrolling its leaves under the bare
trunks of the hickories, ashes, oaks.
All the March air lacks

is a pinch of garlic, and the mustard
has it, just the scent to bring
the bare woods back for an April
feast. We all admire

the innovators, the Japanese
who plant their Prius out on the hybrid
road all by itself. That's garlic
mustard dancing, scattering

seeds, while the staid dandelion
roots down, lays out its leaves,
issues again its standard bloom.
Garlic finds a new

continent, deep shade, oak leaves
where annuals have never hoisted
green flags before. *Invasive*, we say.
Dutifully, I pull up

handfuls of slim stems and pitch
them in handful after handful,
until the dumpster's full. The garlic
exits gracefully.

Its roots are shallow, letting go,
nodding to my zeal, which,
it knows, will wane. Yes, pull
the roots, it says.

You've left some rich, moist soil
loosened up. My seeds
are sleeping there.

Juice in the Pan

Grandmother grips the rooster's legs,
lays his neck
on the bloody stump,

and lifts the axe. Strikes. She tosses
the bird. It runs
in the yard looking for

its head. Not here? Maybe over here?
Then where?
Once around, it drops.

She dips him in scalding water, gets down
to meat, pitches
feathers and feet, takes

the rest inside. An hour gone. Then
out of the oven,
breast, wings, thighs—

newborn, greased and golden, steaming,
juice in the pan.
I wish the hens could see

their man. They'd circle,
spreading their wings.

Divertimento 563

The second movement has had its say.
Time to close it up. Mozart
lets the chords fall in place, they know

their way . . . but no, a detour, a ripple up
then down, backing off
for another stretch of melody

then circling again. He knows
it has to end,
but not till he ornaments

that phrase from the viola, lets the cello
meditate a while
to digest what's just been said—

or at least recall some triplets, some
five-noters, a crooked run
to ease the ear into the sad silence

that will follow. A long-held
chord, the violin
reluctant, wavering. Another

movement's waiting. Mozart steps up
a half note
into a new world and listens.

Vows

The neighbors' rhododendron
seems to have forgotten
how to bloom:

plates of polished leaves
and, in the center,
upright buds,

wrapped, muscular, not
going anyplace, like
high school

linemen, tall on the field,
who never graduate.
Across the road,

those rhododendrons wave their
Kleenex-white diplomas
right on schedule.

Then, one opens here, midnight red.
Those buds weren't linemen,
they were nuns,

closing their hands around
the rosary, renouncing
everything

until those beads murmured
their way out, velvety,
baroque, a color

stolen from a Spanish church
in Cuernavaca, more lush
for waiting,

passion stored in curving sepals
to let it ripen. What vows
do they intend

to keep? The cloister's open now,
tongues and palms and petals
all unfolded,

inviting anything with wings.

Lie and Lay

for Marion

You hear it even in the villanelle—
the subtle elbowing of *lie* and *lay*.
They both go down to bed—so who can tell?

But neither one will wish the other well.
"No transitives in here," cool *lie* will say,
stretched on her sofa in the villanelle.

Lay points out what couples know full well
that *lie* implies some distance—there, away—
when two go down to bed, in parallel.

All seems quiet in stanza four until
lay lets two sensuous voices have their say,
active and passive, nuzzling in the villanelle.

Let's have them both, *lie*, the asphodel
that littered the Elysian Fields, and *lay*,
the drooping blooms of fuchsia on the sill,

each offering its high-tongued syllable
as you and I lie waiting in the hay.
Together they invite the villanelle
to sing, to pass the savory muscatel.

The Savory Wheel

Eight friends at the table, salad
makes the rounds, forks lift rice
and pork. Words

season the meal. Then talk stops—
as though the evening
belonged to the past

that could never be retrieved.

•

Marion waits for the late bus home.
Alone on a Boston corner.

•

I remember the wine—
and cambozola after the show,

two flavors aged, a wedge
from the savory wheel.

•

I slant down to a pocket of water,
scum furring the surface,

everything I've rinsed out
soaking there in the shadowed

scoop of woods. The train
from Morocco, *peligroso*

debajarse on the windowsill,
our oldest daughter, nine,

gone in the night.

•

In Agios Nikolaos, we climb three streets
to the garage where they rent
motorbikes. The salesman is skeptical.

Never ride? He checks with his boss.
Yourself, you drive around block.
He shows me the kick to start it

and the gears. Elbowing traffic, I get
around and back. Marion hops on.
We're Greeks

on the road to the Peloponnese.

•

Outside, plenty of wind to open the hickory
leaves and the waxy bloom
of the azalea.

But here, inside, nothing moves or mutters.
Emptiness is my spouse, attentive,
always ready.

•

Glenn Miller, Tommy Dorsey
at the big hotels downtown.

Marion and Andy jitterbug,
toes twisting, bodies

at arm's length, then slow dance
close as the moan of the sax.

●

Through the screen I watch the past blow by
then find a corner under the stairs
where the future

never thinks to look. Here, out of time, I feel
a hand along my skin, fingers
that once

could empty out an hour, an afternoon,
a cluttered heart.

Algae

Below the steep hill, almost lost
in the trees, is a small lake,
nothing flowing in or out, a handful

of memory left by the last glacier.
Hikers and dog walkers never
look down, so I can claim it.

Whatever I have left
I shrug off, let skid over the fallen
trunks and disappear into

my green bowl. Three mallards
coast in, lower their legs
to clear a landing strip, draw in

their wings, and rest
on the mossy carpet.

•

Those green cells lounging on the water
are generating oxygen and oil. Researchers
speak of pond scum as the holy grail
of biofuels—my Petri dish, my lake.

•

A snake curls from an oak branch,
a red-winged blackbird
waits in the cattails.

Wind lifts a clean breath off
the verdant cells. I let fall
what I can't hold onto anymore,
what was and isn't.

Enormous Leaf

What's real, Whitehead says,
is the moment, taking in
the past, holding it

an instant, passing it on. How to fail?
Close the cupboard, hoard up
what you were

or might have been. It's gone. Another
moment's waiting, hoping for
a twist, a glimpse,

a curious smell, the touch of something
yearning, melting, touching back,
the smallest fresh

invention. From the woods,
an enormous leaf
blows in,

rich brown, two feet across.
I get up and look.
No tree

like that, a moment
without a past.
I finger

the drifting thing.